PRAISE FOR LI(

"*What is it we expect from death?*" Sally Albiso asks in
her poem "After the Neighbor's Dog Dies." In her
final book, *Light Entering My Bones*, she chronicles the
process of dying, the pain of cancer treatment and how
to inhabit a body she knows will not survive. While
she considers mythic biblical figures, how they might
show her how to manage suffering, she does not seek
comfort from a religious perspective on her own death
and dying. Rather, she looks to nature for an order in
which to place herself. In the poem "Fable," she writes,
"*Fireweed grows in the gutters,/moss on the roof,/Spiders
spin their autumnal webs/and my hair begins to fall out.*"
What time she has left, she measures by the rhythms
of the natural world, as if this is the only way she can
inhabit a body that has turned against her: "*I cough up
feathers/and dream of singing/light entering my bones.*"

The poems in the book never descend to self-pity, but
rather find compassion for her husband, the one who
will be left behind. In the poem, "You Cry Upon Hearing
the Diagnosis," she writes, "*Better to be the body desolate
than the eyewitness/tasked with remembering.*" And later
in the poem "Ambulance" she addresses her husband
directly: "*I close my eyes/and am carried farther from you,
husband,/my most faithful disciple.*" At their core, these
are love poems, almost apologetic that he must be both
witness and participant to her dying.

She does not find answers to what to expect from
death, but rather leaves a heartbreaking account of
suffering through a cure she knows will not save her.
And yet, she endures the cure, using what time is left
to her to observe the ironies of nature itself, how life
springs from death, "*like mushrooms on a nurse log.*"

Brave, articulate, with a sharp curiosity, these poems take us step by step through a journey we know will be our own. At times painful to read, you will emerge from the spell of this book with a renewed appreciation and compassion for your own brief life.

~ Karen Whalley, author of
My Own Name Seems Strange to Me

Light
ENTERING MY BONES

Light
ENTERING MY BONES

SALLY ALBISO

MoonPath Press

Poetry
ISBN 978-1-936657-49-0

Cover photo: John Albiso

Author photo: John Albiso

Design: Tonya Namura using
Guess + Guess Sans (display) and Gentium Basic (text)

MoonPath Press is dedicated to publishing the finest poets
of the U.S. Pacific Northwest.

MoonPath Press
PO Box 445
Tillamook, OR 97141

MoonPathPress@gmail.com

http://MoonPathPress.com

This posthumous collection was
arranged by Sally Albiso
just days before she became too
ill to write any longer.

Dedicated to Sally's memory,
may her luminous poems
ever light the way for readers
everywhere.

ACKNOWLEDGMENTS

Thank you to the following journals in which some of the poems in this collection first appeared:

"Birds Reside in Me" — Autumn 2019 issue *The Bitter Oleander*

"Five Cosmological Headlines, First Person Accounts" — Fall 2019 issue *BoomerLit Mag*

"Genesis" — December 2018 issue *2 River View*

"Rendition" — Fall 2019 issue *BoomerLit Mag*

"Road Trip" — Fall 2019 issue *BoomerLit Mag*

"A Struggle with Time" — Fall 2019 issue *BoomerLit Mag*

CONTENTS

III. A MANNER OF DEVOTION

IV. INSTRUCTIONS FOR SURVIVING

INTRODUCTION TO
LIGHT ENTERING MY BONES
BY SALLY ALBISO

When I think of her, it's in scenes. She's at Studio Bob's during an exhibit of student art. She's sitting across from me at a restaurant lunch. Or I see her at a friend's birthday celebration, poetry readings at Peninsula College and Northwind Gallery. Sally, who was an artist with words, whom I imagine reading this as I write, taught to go in fear of abstraction—to conjure fresh language, to push through to higher levels to express what feels so inexpressible. But in writing this introduction to an irreplaceable friend and poet, I'm reminded of Dante trying to describe Paradiso, how he felt humanly and poetically inadequate. I picture Sally sending me an email in red-font track-changes suggesting I've overreached resurrecting Dante's task as I write this appreciation of her.

We were poetry writing partners for eight years, critiquing poems via email. Beginning the process tentatively as two people will when starting a new writing relationship, we tested how sensitive or immune we might be to each other's critical reading of our work. Not knowing each other's approach, how were we to know if one or the other might hide stones in snowballs? But we soon grew comfortable with each other—Sally's suggestions always direct and straightforward and honest, and because of this, her enthusiasm regarding a poem that moved her felt genuine. A highlight in my writing life happened when I opened an attachment from her and read her latest offering.

Our exchange began the year I retired from Peninsula College, ecstatic at owning my hours and having time to write. One day after a Foothills Series reading—the featured poet must have been Tess Gallagher—I talked to Sally and her husband, John, as we waited for the audience to thin. I knew Sally was a poet but didn't know much more. We discussed the lyrical narratives we'd just heard where ideas and images were woven in surprising and startling warp and weft, how loose threads of association merged into whole cloth. *That's how I want to write*, Sally expressed, her eyes so alive in the dim light of the Little Theatre. What I didn't know was that weaving associations was how she wrote her poems. When she suggested we share work, I knew I'd found something worth cultivating: someone willing to review half-realized poems, someone focused and serious. Over the years our work came to involve much more. We shared poets we'd discovered—Jude Nutter one of Sally's, Maryann Corbett one of mine. We shared a palette of forms and devices and experiments. We shared the acceptances of our work for publication, and we shared the rejections. We'd finish our critiques with *Send me a poem.*

Before I worked one-on-one with Sally and until her death, she was a member of the North Coast Writers, a long-standing group whose friendship in poetry extended beyond the workshop. Suzann Bick, Mary-Alice Boulter, Patrick Loafman, Diana Somerville, and others who moved on are among the writers who sustained each other and encouraged Sally's work, evolving in their fiction, nonfiction, and poetry through Sally's participation. As one member wrote, "After... she read her contribution for [the workshop], it left us...[with] pure pleasure—and sometimes shivering at the dark that could lurk within." It's true that among Sally's poems that celebrate this sweet ride of life, darkness also inhabits her work—poems addressing the suffering inherent in the world. The poems chronicling the cancer that stole her life burn with this honesty and truth.

But there is also an abundance of *light*, a word appearing frequently in these poems. Shortly before her death, she told me Judaism is vague on the afterlife—how it might be a place of unending darkness—or unending light. When I think of Sally, I remember the light I saw in her eyes that day in the Little Theater, and I think of lines from her poem "Conversation":

I...imagine...recurring as a tide so moons govern my surge, the sun penetrates my depths.

So you see. There is light.

Carmen Germain
Port Angeles, Washington
07 February 2020

Light ENTERING MY BONES

I.

Hard
ACHE

YOU CRY UPON HEARING THE DIAGNOSIS

though I'm the sick one. Better
to be the body desolate than the eyewitness
tasked with remembering. Do you recall

the dog that followed us on a walk,
too weak to raise her tail in greeting,
to do more than stumble behind?

How a shock collar hung from her neck,
the escape she risked, the street
empty as an arena pending its spectacle.

So tired, the dog panted, *Thirsty*
and trailed us to the corner where we feared
for her safety, walked faster so she couldn't

keep pace. You told me not to look back,
that someone would find her,
hind legs collapsing. Later that summer,

my tumor was revealed. You cried in the hospital
elevator where a stranger offered his hand
and in the waiting room where a woman sat close,

wept for anyone who might console.
I waited for lions. Better to be sacrificed
than charged with testament,

to be the martyr and not the one lamenting—
loss surviving longer in memory
than in flesh. I think of the dog.

How her feet splayed and she fell once
struggling to get up. How she still followed
as we ran.

HARD ACHE

Like all the world's sorrow
is gathered beneath my breasts:
a tautness of muscle
that can't be released.

Bile escapes my mouth
as if the entrance to Hades.
What's mined deep in the gut
and brought to the surface,

pain I'm asked to quantify
on a scale of one to ten:
more than watching the news?
less than a bird dying in my hands?

I curl, an apostrophe
indicating possession
yet own nothing but this ache.
What could be gall

calcified into stone,
which must be pushed
Sisyphus-like from the body—
or the pancreas, the liver

turning on itself.
For weeks, this burn
as if the Sacred Heart of Jesus
aflame with love.

BIRDS RESIDE IN ME

I cough up feathers
and dream of singing,
light entering my bones.
Ruby-crowned kinglets
flutter about my heart like valves
while gulls keen in my liver
like heirs feigning grief.
They want more of everything.

I open my mouth
so blackbirds lining my stomach
escape. How they call all day,
crowd the feeder, dark and slick
as if brushed with butter.
I'd bake them in a pie, brown their cries
beneath a flaky crust
until the house smells

of caramelized need,
the sweet scent of the satiated—
but I've only this throat
and a voice that fades.
When kingfishers dive
into my bloodstream
to gather platelets like fish,
I begin to bruise, contusions

decorating my body in the shape
of shadowed swimming. I scratch
at skin's surface as if it were water
through which salt rises, take deep breaths
and submerge beneath sleep

while grosbeaks peck at the suet
between my ribs, an ache
like being elbowed aside.

SIDE EFFECTS

Nausea, vomiting, diarrhea.
Fatigue, joint pain, mouth sores.
Hair loss, weight loss,

fever. I focus on body temperature
and will it to cool, think arctic, polar bears,
melting sea ice?

Aren't fevers supposed to be starved
not bears with fur like city snow
sullied by exhaust? The thermometer

registers higher yet within acceptable
limits. The bears understand
to cover their dark noses with a paw

while hunting seals, to listen
for surfacing shadows
though they can't make floes freeze.

I understand the need to eat
though food reminds me of whale blubber,
an acquired taste. A dietician suggests

marijuana oil, two drops under the tongue
before meals, insists
there's no accompanying high.

But has she tested it—
giggled while seated at the table,
become paranoid about forks and knives?

How we're taught to sit upright
and spoon our soup out to sea.
Learn how to stab, to cut.

BLOODY NOSE

Pink-tinged mucous when I blow,
a muted hemorrhage
like a silent film star weeping.

We stop at a traffic signal
where naked mannequins pose
in an empty storefront,

palms cupping air.
How bare their mouths look
without speech as the red light sets

their plastic lips ablaze
and a weak capillary in my nose
gives way. So many vessels within me

growing smaller and smaller. I lick marrow
from bones, would divine auspices
but the entrails are gone.

FABLE

Fireweed grows in the gutters,
moss on the roof.
Spiders spin their autumnal webs
and my hair begins to fall out.

I weave a mourner's memento,
place some strands beneath my pillow
so a prince climbs the tower
of my dreams, rescues a balding heroine—

no rope of braid to let down,
only the pale tangle of my arms.
We could escape to a distant castle
far from wizards with their infusions

and he'd knit me a hat from his locks,
a poultice from his breath
that makes hair return dense as lichen.
Or shave his own pate,

another moon rising
as we make oblations to the stars—
gather novas on our tongues
like prayer beads

so latent fire fills our mouths,
the vacuity of space. Such stillness there
like the hand of God reaching
but not quite touching Adam's.

TO HAVE EYEBROWS LIKE FRIDA KAHLO'S

A dark abundance like a telephone wire
dense with crows. A glut where forehead meets gaze,
hirsute stare from which others can't look away.
Something to groom and create the illusion
of oneness. How the sky might seem less bald then,
my scalp, though I fear brows and lashes
will also go and I'll resemble the Mona Lisa:
my regard bared to the world, the question
of my smile. Whether it implies amusement
or perplexity at being singled out.

*

To have eyebrows like Frida Kahlo's,
a querying hedge I stroke like a beard
and appear wise. That I'm listening,
to all the oncologist says
while my eyes stare darkly
and he palpates my abdomen like a soothsayer
studying auspices. Beyond the windowless room,
there are mountains named for Olympus.
There's water that boats ceaselessly ply
as if ferrying souls across the river Styx.

PIGEON MAN

His home is the sidewalk
by the parking garage for the hospital.
Pieces of bread surround him

like a doughy frost and his flock
with one gull presiding.

It's raining. The man's sleeping bag is wet,
the slurry of bread crumbs
yet his faithful don't abandon him,

their feathers turning from pale to dark
like the sky, their red gaze.

They pace the pavement. They coo
and he answers them,
understands the language of birds.

Whenever we visit the hospital, he's there
and I would trade places with him—

live on the street and scatter bread
for those who fly rather than be tethered
to drugs meant to destroy the wayward

in me. The birds disperse and settle again.
The man remains still

beneath his blanket of crumbs.
This is his house of cardboard, this his brood
to gather and tend.

A convocation of wings,
heavenly host he serves with his torn offering.

AMBULANCE

Speed, siren, flashing lights
like a train at a railroad crossing,
a carnival ride obeying no traffic signals.

It's late. I imagine a few cars
pulling over and giving affliction its due

as if something holy. I'm not
outside with them speculating
about accidents or heart attacks

but inside strapped to a gurney.
An EMT ministers, attentive as an acolyte,

and a driver races to reach the last ferry.
Out the back windows, retreating road
oily with rain, aura of streetlights,

the slumbering world. I close my eyes
and am carried farther from you, husband,

my most faithful disciple. In the morning,
an obstructed duct will be opened
so bile will flow freely again

and be passed by the body—a struggle
to live without bitterness.

FORTY-SIX HOURS

How long this infusion lasts—
a pump like another heart I'll sleep with
and become full of what kills. Learn to lie

on my back and dream of floating
or curl on one side, still as a sock
left behind in a drawer. But it's hard to drift

with no water beneath me
and what good is one sock? A sequestering
that yearns for the embrace of soles.

Two dusks, two dawns
before the pump empties.
How we're mostly surface, mostly sleeve

and skin such frail protection
for what rests beneath. I splay on the bed,
taste salt as if washing out to sea

like the remains of uprooted trees—
their trunks waterlogged,
their branches still reaching for sky.

HE LOWERS THE DOSE

by twenty-five percent when I complain
about dry heaving,
that I can't eat through the nausea and diarrhea.
A fine line between killing me versus the cancer.
How I might starve first.

My doctor wears purple to celebrate the pancreas he treats
and Jerry Garcia ties. A Deadhead back in the day,
he's portly with his own appetite.
Does he worry too? How anyone can succumb

though he's a kind of god who mitigates punishment
at will. He lowers the dose so I suffer less,
gain an ounce or two, hosanna, a pound.
When he proffers an appetite stimulant like an apple,

I say yes: knowledge its own scale of plus and minus
to balance the growth unfurled within me
like the heartiest of perennials, roots reaching.
He palpates my abdomen, listens to my heart.

I admire his tie, the patrician shades of lavender, plum,
amethyst he sports beneath his white coat,
pristine as a wedding gown. The belief
in measured promises. The oath he took to do no harm.

COLOR WHEEL

Home for days at a time, each window my horizon,
each room my field of wheat,
I cull the stairs and pace the hall,

a kind of gleaning. I take a shower
and recognize my body though smaller in proportion
and freer of hair on head, legs, pudenda—

slough off soap, feel the pulse of water
on my back and have no need to go out
grown used to walls, the light skirting them.

I eat every few hours in an attempt
to gain weight though I'd prefer to become less,
to lift into the ether untethered from flesh.

When I travel to the city for treatment,
I miss home, the bed with its new comforter
in shades of orange and blue

van Gogh would have recognized as complementary:
his own bed *chrome yellow*, pillows and sheets
green-citron, blanket *blood red*.

His room in Arles, in the house where he hoped
Gauguin would join him and create a refuge
from want. But the house too small

to contain them, they argued
about painting from memory or from sight,
faces flaring like the ear van Gogh severed

in his fury and fear of abandonment.
The iron-barred window of his cell at Saint-Paul's
limiting his view of the sky

so he painted a starry night from memory.
Its white pulse and the black reach of a cypress
composing another complementary pair

like when I rouse myself to wear lipstick
and enter the world:
the darkness of my mouth, my pale face.

THE LOVESICK WITCH

I don't want the body, she whimpered.
It hurts.
      ~ Anne Bishop

After chemo in the city hours away:
one ferry, one bridge to cross,
your left hand curls around the steering wheel
while mine grips a pen. Sinister
how ink stains me like the drugs in my veins.
Will I be accused of sorcery
forced to swim damned either way?
Drowning the proof of virtue
and survival my mastery of dark arts.
The potion I'll concoct to enhance allure
despite my denuding. My hand imprinted
with spells so you always love me
and night resounds with your need: a cat's yowl,
a fingernail scraping stars from the sky.

WINTER,

though one rhododendron flowers and birds sing
as if it were March not January. The sun warms them enough
to stake territory; I pretend it's hot on my belly
and burns away the cramping there.
When we take walks, the birds accompany us
and it seems spring will soon follow, the surgery
where most of my pancreas is removed, my stomach
and gallbladder I'll digest without
as if gall will no longer plague me. The birds chorus,
a waste of energy, misplaced hope?
Already days lengthen and the horizon swells
with light. When we eat supper, more than our faces
reflect in the windows and two seasons of diagnosis
behind me—this winter when birds sing.

*

This winter when birds sing, my tumor *kisses*
a major artery. It must shrink or be left behind. No cure
for what bleeds. But if it rounds into a smaller sphere
and is taken all of a piece the way night swallows song—
my abdomen will empty like the sky lowering toward dusk,
organs parsed so no cancer remains.
How it hid within me, maybe for years,
silent as most birds in January.
How it tests the limits of the season, its nest.

*

Testing the limits of its nest, the malignancy
could be a bird desperate to find a mate.
It ignores the cold onslaught of chemo
and warbles of annuals returning.
Golden-crowned sparrows flock to the suet, the Pacific wren.

They raise their voices despite the fear of hawks
overhead. They are outrageous in their need
to be heard. I call to you—
don a coat, gloves, hat for my denuded head.
It's always winter when you have little hair
though my eyebrows and eyelashes remain.
I fill them in with pencil where they've thinned,
a vanity so my face has some dimension,
wear lipstick. The birds wear their drab feathers.
Only their voices are exultant, a little sun all they need
to herald spring as the bare branches of trees
brave wind. Months before they leaf,
before I learn whether the growth in me can be removed
while one rhododendron burgeons with blooms.

LETTER

Dear Tumor,

How was your vacation? Six weeks with no chemotherapy
and a whole beach to yourself. Did you enjoy
the solitude, no assaults to parry?
Now your sabbatical's at an end
as we start radiation.
Then we'll see who shrinks to nothing
like the Wicked Witch of the West, who burns.
You nap like a cat that hunts nights
and never stops seeking prey:
intrude on nerves as if gnashing teeth at birds.
I imagine incisors crunching through bone
and paws with nails that don't retract.

Evenings are the worst. Those few hours after dinner
when we watch TV and pain bleeds
through my narcotic haze.
I'm unable to control you then: must suffer your rousing
as if you're auditioning for a reality show.
Just so you know, a course of radiation
and you'll be removed at last.
The intent of this letter is *goodbye*.
How you're about to become discarded pathology
and I your host only until your last reveling cell dies.

LOL,

S.

CUT

1

Men with chainsaws climb forty feet,
shear the branches off a cedar
until only a naked trunk remains
allowing the eye to travel over water and sky
as if only distance matters
and what's seen close blurs like the image
in an ultrasound. That diffused floating
as when fog conceals the boughs of firs.
I fear for the tree trimmers' limbs, for the tree—
heart ringed with the widening
and narrowing of years
and the wounds saws leave.

2

There was a time when some were born
without limbs, a void
where an appendage should be,
just head and trunk emerging
like ancient statuary:
Hermes without winged feet,
Artemis without hands to draw a bow.
How a drug can sever what branches
sure as a saw. My former neighbor
with his plastic right arm, a hook.
When he reached, it flashed like a knife
and remained a perilous hold.
To balance absence, he walked
with a prosthetic left leg.

3

I was delivered with all my members,
only the unseen severed from me:
uterus, lumps in breasts.
I've escaped malignancy until now—
the pancreas rebelling, tired
of producing insulin and digestive enzymes
creating a tumor instead.
One at its head not its tail
so discovered before metastasizing
and borderline removable.
We keep testing its margins.
Whether it still branches close
to a major artery or roots around it
like mushrooms on a nurse log.

4

The tree trimmers continue their work.
They hook themselves to ropes.
My neighbor had a hook for a hand,
could bite into bark.

5

Will the first slice be the hardest?
The incising into skin as if it were bark,
organs like branches carefully pruned
so the trunk is preserved
and the prospect improved.

No signs of tumor left, no cells forking
to the colon, the liver.
A scar from breast bone to belly button
as proof of limbing. How tidy my insides
will be. How much better the view.

LULLABY

I have ... on my easel the portrait of a woman ...
rocking the cradle ... a lullaby in colours ...
~ Vincent van Gogh

You sing me to sleep
as the moon pulls trees to its chin
and floats deeper toward the chanting of stars.

You paint my dreams with your voice
so I can see the cobalt in night's lament,
pale tenor of an owl's flight

shivering beneath my lids.
You sing me the colors of darkness
as I turn my face from you

and leave my body behind like reverie.
Come morning, roses beyond the window
hemorrhage light. You hum

of purples and oranges
and all the flaming sunrise's swirl.
My cheeks burgeon with pink

and chartreuse, mouth blooms
like the scales and feathers
announcing fish and birds:

their stripes, spots,
prismatic tails
protection against predatory gray.

When you croon my lips turquoise,
you should recognize my smile
as a warning.

CONVERSATION

When we speak, it's about our bodies.
The wearing away of tissue
until nothing's left but bone on bone, deep pockets
beneath molars. We want assurance

that we'll live shadowed by the same self
as ten years ago, twenty. That we can turn from
the unraveling in mirrors.
That my tumor will shrink enough to remove.
And if it doesn't, we can converse about souls.

Of a dreamless afterlife full of undiminished darkness
or light. How you remain hopeful
knees, teeth, cancer can be remedied
and I grow more silent, imagine returning as a snail,

silver traces left behind me to mark time.
Or recurring as a tide so moons govern my surge,
the sun penetrates my depths. I could pace Earth
as an elephant and trumpet like an annunciating angel.

A guardian who sits on shoulders and whispers counsel
to others through sorrow long ago named.
You talk and my bones hear.
There are choices to be made.

I ignore the newly revealed spot on my liver
and think of Paris. How we've never been there
together, that city for lovers and dogs.
The streets mined with shit trailed into the Louvre

where the Mona Lisa muses with tired smile
as if she smells it too.
I think of rioting students drunk on new wine
and demanding more—roads littered with glass,
splintered bottles opening like throats—

and when I wanted something that much.
On our rendezvous in Marseilles? How I dreamed
in full sun, body parallel to yours,
listened to what the sea advised. When to come closer.

When to subside. Was it then I last felt no fear?
Before a plane brought me home
through a summer storm, lightning limned my profile
and nothing but water below to break the fall.

You talk and my blood rises,
ears prick like a horse's, nostrils flare.
We'll test in another month's time.
Until then I'm free to forget my body's undoing

and keep pain to three or four
on a scale of one to ten. So hard to quantify
when up against the world's litany of grief.
To meet your eyes and see the unmeasurable there.

II.

Chaos THEORY

BRETHREN

You are making a relative of the crow, the one
that frequents our suet and awaits other handouts:
stale pieces of bread it soaks in the bird bath,
a dead robin who broke its neck on our windows.

The crow knows you now as friend not foe
and doesn't fear your shadow.
Maybe you'll become corvid, darken
about the face with feathers, flock west

each night. You'll leave me and roost among trees
while I remain pinioned under sheets
dreaming of flight. How it would feel
to gain lift with only air beneath.

If you begin to caw in warning when I approach,
we'll have to talk. Maybe I could become corvid
too, reward the crow with bits of food
from my plate, habituate it to my face,

lunar in its rise to fullness. Then the black
of its gaze would turn to me
and I'd be favored with acknowledgment,
learn to fold my arms into wings

and gleam in the sun like another daystar.
To wash what I'm given like a host to be blessed
and learn who to trust, who to avoid.
Would you stay with me then and not fly

from our bed but bury your head beneath down
until the crow visits again? How readily
it's taken to you, a little kindness going far,
and you to it as if always part bird, part scavenger.

CATTLE IN MOONLIGHT

offer their bulk to each other,
turn from the fence that contains them
to face a pasture of sky
lavish with stars.

The cattle shift and low,
breath mingling with fear
when a rabbit screams then is still
making its short life known.

They huddle
beneath the moon's waxing
while coyotes celebrate its fullness,
a coin of light to be spent

among shadows. The dark smells
of manure and rotting apples
deer devour where they fall
as if nothing is forbidden.

Eat, I whisper.
There are no angels here
with flaming swords
and no other Eden.

CHAOS THEORY

The day so hot even poultry is panting:
chickens and turkeys with open beaks,

throats pulsing as if oven doors are closing in
and feathers fluttering wildly
beneath fans. We move on

to watch the hypnotist convince people they're cold.
Such shivering as another subject falls in love

with the stranger to his left. He's on his knees
proffering a ring made of air. She finds him repulsive

as suggested and swats at the mosquito whine
of his fervor. Meanwhile, in the pig barn,

long-suffering sows nurse ten piglets at once,
their devotion not unlike lovesickness:

the swelling tenderness, supine patience,
all those mouths.
And what of the cows, udders stretched taut as desire?

How they must dream of release,
calves taken away so we drink the milk instead,

or that of goats who resemble Zen masters:
horizontal pupils seeing ahead and behind them,

not blinded by light from above.
How we sway at the Ferris wheel's apex

as heat from the midway rises like screams
from the Tilt-A-Whirl and fairgoers revel in motion

that can't be predicted: the direction and speed
of each spinning car dependent on
its passengers' weight.

Those who could startle when a butterfly lands,
shift the load and change everything.

FIVE COSMOLOGICAL HEADLINES, FIRST PERSON ACCOUNTS

Salmon Leap in the Sky and Floods Begin

What's mistaken for fast moving clouds
are fish swimming through air
and massed on the horizon like storm.
Daily, small bones pour down
and are caught in throats.
Some swallow them whole. Some choke,
refuse to go outside until the sun brightens.
Either way, arched skeletons
are the only constellations rising
and we imagine natal streams:
sweeping gravel into nests and laying eggs,
depositing milt. The salmon hurdle lunar currents.
Flooding reaches new heights,
offerings made to shadowed noon.
But how much blood will raise light again,
release the blue in sea and sky, the prostrate trees
from weeping. We take comfort in old ways:
build arks, gather animals—
our voices hushed by wild refrain—
fashion fish to worship, their scales burnished
as overlapping stars. Yet salmon orbit
and the deluge continues.
Hills shake their sodden coats like dogs.
A dove appears with ladders of bone in its beak.

Dog Takes Moon into Her Mouth

She drags it to ground with her howl,
pads down hallways, lips the orb softly,
a bird she's retrieved. We who slumber
begin to stir, observe the sky's void,

each hour darkening. We wake
to find the moon burning
where the dog dropped it whining for reward.
Though she was christened *Luna*
and we call for the moon daily,
we insist she put its radiance back
spilling everywhere. She howls
the moon skyward again
as a screech owl chalks night's blackboard.
We who woke return to dreams.
The dog gums a remnant of light, true to her name.

Stars Refuse to Shine

They're tired of brightening a world
that clings to darkness.
We'll leave it to the trees,
the stellae whisper in voices that burn:
Let the rooted rise and fill the sky
with hoarded light.
So ornamental plums bloom pink
to enhance dawn and dusk.
Coconut palms release their seeds into orbit
pulled like satellites toward the rind of Earth.
And among groves of redwoods, trunks explode
into novas, no damping such coals.
What stars linger nod like sages,
stroke their beards of latent flame.

Astronaut Chooses to Remain in Space

A pinprick of light, the comet tail
of her tether floating loose, lure
of severing attachments—
she weightlessly watches the sun rise and set
before oxygen runs out.

Does she seek an infinite silence?
Freedom from voices held fast by gravity?
She drifts close to Venus to understand love,
circles Saturn like one of its rings—
becomes a particle of ice,
small as a salt grain, large as a house.
The message she left quoting Genesis:
and it was evening and it was morning, one day.

Sightings of Extraterrestrials Increase

Aliens with skin so thick it can't be pierced
and hearts so efficient they don't break.
With multiple eyes like insects to catch movement
from behind and blood that denotes emotion:
sky blue for calm, orange excitement, grey sorrow.
Hominids who walk upright like us
but speak telepathically,
a ringing in the ears we've yet to decipher.
Some insist these beings are angels
though they have no trumpets,
no flaming swords. They simply appear
and allow us to study them.
Or remain invisible, evident only
by what they act upon: a sudden flailing
of trees, while no wind, higher tides.
Some predict the end of times, others the beginning.

GENESIS

A late snowstorm,
an unexpected chill.
Hours of circling in place,
of nosing windows like dogs.
How we might tongue joy
but conserve heat, the power out.
Headlamps light our faces,
worn between the eyes
like phylacteries.
Clocks flash twelve,
a tribal count no matter the hour.
The woodstove ticks
and we play Scrabble
though few synonyms
for this hush. *Brittle*
would be most accurate.
How solidity is illusion
and time splinters like bone.
If I steal your lowest rib,
will I become another woman?
One who never shivers.
Who knows all the words for sorrow
yet wins.

I BELIEVE IN ANGELS,
YOU ROLL YOUR EYES

That a presence descended beneath a shelter of wings
and pulsed with light, which confused yipping coyotes
and woke me to radiance as I knelt.
The being wafted through a window luster spilling,
wings puddling on the floor like drapes.
If she'd fanned them, they would have filled the room
and at rest cast a shadow like a plane.
I squinted at her face, her gaze steady as a child's,
folded my hands in obeisance, bowed my head
and thought about the coin in my wallet
engraved with an angel's likeness. What had come
with a cancer appeal, a gift to encourage giving.
A friend received the same coin and presented it to me
in a box he carved. *Coincidence*, you insist,
though I keep it on my nightstand as a talisman,
earthly representation of the divine.
You protest you never woke, didn't see anything.
But belief may be a prerequisite to such sight.
Circular reasoning, you sniff. I remember feathers
littering the bed, each plume two feet long,
the messenger's white-hot light.
What about the devil? you ask.
Does your credence include the fallen?
The devil is cartoonish to me, fictional evil
meant to scare us toward atonement. A tradition
of heaven and hell I wasn't raised with—
good behavior its own reward and bad its own punishment.
The angel whispered of milk and honey.
I rose and led her to the kitchen, downy cape dragging
down the hall. The honey melted at her touch
and milk thickened into cream,
the elegant span of her throat worked.
A dream, you still insist when I recount how she folded

41

onto the floor as if to rest and I crouched
to examine where her wings grew
from her shoulder blades—
a rawness there and oozing skin as if she were infected
with the world's suppurating wounds. You roll your eyes.

MISPLACED

I am out with lanterns, looking for myself.
    ~ Emily Dickinson

My night vision suffers and what's mistaken for
an arm, a hand are the denuded branches of alders,
roosting crows. I return to the house and begin
a room-to-room search. The kitchen takes days:
all those dishes examined for a reflection,
the cutlery. In each cupboard and drawer
an answering silence, I pace the hall
though my shadow doesn't and enter the bathroom
where mirrors reveal nothing.
Ever hopeful, I proceed to the bedroom. Surely some
semblance of self rests among the sheets:
an impression where my head shaped a pillow,
dreams of trains coming and going, unrecognized faces
at windows. Onto the living room where only light
sprawls and an outline of my body is chalked
on the floor, spine visible like that of fish discovered
at great depths. The woodstove fills with ash.
I go back outside to rummage in the trash,
look for myself among the discarded.

SO MANY ENDEARMENTS

We were together. I forget the rest.
  ~ Walt Whitman

Did you call me luz as if my mouth cupped the sun,
take my hand, place it on your pulse and whisper
corazón? Did you take me to see men fight bulls
in suits of light, get down on their knees
before lowered horns and the crowd's avowal?
Did I close my eyes to their shadows,
bite my tongue so I tasted blood? Did you
murmur *dulzura* as if my mouth savored honey,
cielo as if I contained the sky,
mi vida, mi alma—insist
passion would always be a dusty arena,
afternoons turning to bone,
heat at the edges of shuttered windows?
Did a gypsy woman read my palms and sigh?

A STRUGGLE WITH TIME

the indefinite continued progress of existence . . .
~ Wikipedia

It's always been this way.
If someone says three o'clock, I think nine.
If they describe the bow of a boat
as twelve, the stern as six
and all the hours in between,
I look in the wrong direction
and miss the breaching whale.

I labor over number-bearing
cards, can't keep hands straight:
flushes, full houses.
My house is full of missing hearts
like the skipped pulse
when a phone rings too late,
family calling or a stranger

transposing a digit. I could converse
about false moves, answer loss
but usually talk over another voice,
unsure how long to pause
between responses,
to distinguish clockwise
from counterclockwise.

I'd pay attention to shadows,
the chiaroscuro of Renaissance masters.
But here whole weeks with little sun
and the contrast is obscured,
no telling dawn from dusk.
A twenty-four hour clock helps:
adding twelve to each hour

like disciples of time
distinguishing the treachery of night
from that of daybreak.
Yet minutes still confuse, the shift
of hands at *before* as opposed to *after*,
while behind my back,
whales leap from water.

OWNERSHIP

The feral cat sprays to mark what's his:
brush, grass, the world
while nothing belongs to me.

Not flesh, bone, wind over water.
Not my shadow in its slow remove.

The cat stalks birds,
possesses perimeters of light,
flight he'd cup in his mouth.

I voice custody
yet nothing belongs to me.

Not my stuttering sight or pulse,
my heart that could stiffen into a fist
clutching its sanguine palm.

A sparrow might throb as well
beneath the breast, flailing wings.

The cat keeps to the shadows,
possesses the sky.
When I clap my hands in warning,

birds grow still but the predator remains
where he is owning sorrow.

VENUE

Vultures lately fill my days.
They circle and rain down
among cedars, hunch
shoulder to shoulder

and preen their dark vestments.
They are patient jurors,
the indicting blush
of their featherless heads. In our courtroom,

the prosecutor sports a red tie,
though not yet bald,
and the defendant wears gray
like a winter sky.

But there's no hiding.
She is only one and we are twelve
arguing like dissenting gulls
while the vultures silently maintain

their verdict. Yet how to determine the truth
beyond reasonable doubt?
To judge another's heart
while plucking out their eyes?

WHAT BROKE

A mother, a wrist,
both fractures aching

as clouds splinter distance
like dropped glass

and flesh no longer keeps
its footing.

Buoys washed onto the beach
lashed to nothing but sand.

Voices on the phone
and each nimbus of light

hovering above
bowed heads.

A dam, houses downstream.
More glass, other bones.

The tablets held aloft
in Moses' arms.

AT THE LIBRARY

Night has been dusted from shelves
and books wait for their pages to be turned,
newspapers to imprint hands
with some measure of truth. People speak softly
as if babies nap among the stacks
and will startle into consciousness,
stiffen like the spines of hardbacks
expecting to be held. How words can rest for years
before stirring like the homeless who also sleep here,
one woman in layers of multihued coats
as if she interprets dreams. Whether we wake
to punishment or mercy—her lips moving
in silent prophecy, her feet bared
to anyone who might kneel and wash them.

WHEN THE SNOW FALLS

and stars congeal, plummeting to earth
in frigid descent, we go out to greet them.
We make angels of our bodies
and petition the stellae to remain with us.

But they melt back into the sky
and only a distant spark is left to wish upon.
It will be years before they clot again.
This time we eat some

and our mouths fill with coals.
We roll them into spheres to preserve
and they take on the tint
of graying meat. They flare to ash

as dusk balances the moon on its back
and we're forced to acknowledge grace,
which never lasts long
and smells of blood.

COLD

A new ice age
where the living grow so pale
we walk among ghosts
and color fades from memory
as eyes forget to distinguish
night from day—

each hour a little less heat
and only so much wood.
When the trees disappear,
we burn the furniture.
A bed frame, a table
little good when sleep eludes

from too much shivering
and the scarcity of food.
How the sun rises gelid as a moon
and we describe snow like the Inuit:
drifting or still, marked by wolves,
carried on breath. A tomb for the dead.

Some turn to old religions,
gods of fire. Melt jewelry into idols
with gilded hooves
and horns that curve skyward
as if to part the heavens,
reveal our star. Some cut themselves

for blood offerings, flower red.
But winter persists, our one season.
The sun arcs lower
and we suck the marrow
from bones, repeat—like a mantra—
the antonyms for *cold.*

FAIRY TALES I TELL MYSELF

Wind all day huffing at the house,
wily and strong. It insinuates
around corners and pants at the roof,
harasses the bay until waves froth white
as frantic sheep, their hooves
that never touch land.

Each hour drags its light
before me, contracting and expanding
like a stove's metallic tick.
The dark thickens.
The moon replaces its mantle
and stars bank their distant fires.

I feel an eyelash drop
onto a cheek, the cheek's response,
and light candles as if honoring my dead.
Still the wind increases,
might blow the house down
as windows shiver like glass slippers

and clocks flash twelve.
That hour of transformation
when I forego any hopes of a prince
and take to the woods to confront
my toothy predator: his stink of undigested flesh
and flowers I gathered for grandmother.

HOW TO LEAVE THE BODY BEHIND

First, remove all appendages:
arms, elbows, wrists, hands;
legs, knees, ankles, feet. Stow them
in the back of a closet
where hands can pet your faux fur coat
and feet stuff themselves into heels.
With only a trunk and head left,
you can start to dispose of remaining flesh,
organs parceled like pieces of mail:
heart to New Jersey and liver to Kentucky,
kidneys landing somewhere farther west.
The pancreas and intestines also recycled,
corneas, mouths. As for your head,
it can be saved even if faceless:
sit on a shelf like a wig stand and stare blindly
while you're freed of its weight, the brain's chatter.
Such silence like the time before time
and no perimeters of bone but ribs
arching toward where your heart once beat.
How valuable you'll be stripped—
grin lifting a stranger's countenance,
eyes reflecting another's gaze.

ROAD TRIP

You take me where I've never been:
asphalt humming into distance,

carved faces of presidents, graves
of soldiers buried where they fell.

We cross wind-shocked plains
where you once hunted rabbits,

their hind legs still kicking as they dropped.
Where tornadoes tore at the horizon

and you hid in cellars among shelves
of preserves, tomatoes suspended like hearts

in glass jars while outside fury threatened
as if winged monkeys filled the sky.

The stillness after, cicadas trilling
among furrows of corn.

Each farmhouse, barn, dog
gnawing at shadows, we reach lakes

that look like seas, sniff the air for salt.
You hold my hand so I remain balanced,

the need for equilibrium, staying upright.
Some days, calls of wolves

like a train whistle growing faint.
Other days, badgers shambling along tracks

as if riding the rails like men my mother called
hobos, who were always on the move.

Those who knocked on back doors.
Whose hands shook when she gave them bread.

What will you give me as we return west:
answers to questions like coyotes ask of night?

Whether morning will bring enough light?
Whether it's safe to be alive?

III.

A
Manner
OF DEVOTION

AFTER THE NEIGHBOR'S DOG DIES

we find a bone of hers
on our cat's grave.
An offering that wasn't there before,
a gift from the spirit world.
This is our explanation
for its appearance.
This is how we manage grief.

*

Another week, and a jay
hunches on the ground
like an old man,
his blue suit and black fedora
gone limp. Two days he lingers
then is gone, a Greek chorus
of cats in the night.
Yet no plucked down,
no bundle of bones
greet light. Your theory,
the jay was carried off whole,
mine, he overcame injury and flew.
For I want to believe in mercy,
in the creed of flight,
the holy ghost of wind.

*

What is it we expect from death—
bones the measure of loss,
headstones it takes years
for weather to round?
Here, a baby awaiting his parents
as if not yet born,

there, husbands awaiting their brides
like patient grooms.
And on a hill, soldiers
lost to war. So many,
we call out names taking muster.
We walk on upturned faces.

*

After the neighbor's dog dies,
two bucks visit,
antlers not yet forked.
They chase each other
and mock fight.
They romp unafraid:
no canine scent, no bark
and time yet
before they become trophies
or must challenge for dominance.
They're alive and free from sorrow.
How we envy them.

BIRTHDAY CARD

We're now the same age, your spine collapsing
while my hips weaken.
So much brittle in us, we could splinter like glass
and shine among rocks
until someone collects our shards,
pale as fog among the amber
of broken bottles. We could be swallowed by gulls
and taken to sea in their crops, still sharp enough
to slice or tumbled to a milky finish
like eyes veiled by cataracts.
We could stoop beneath
the weight of years,
forced to turn our heads to see peripherally,
call to each other
in the voices of prophets
and predict what our bones will do next.
I enclose a gift of powdered marrow.
Put it in tea to thicken
against fracturing.
When you visit, we'll walk the beach
and look for ourselves among the shattered.

LIFESPAN

In each window a web
and the remains of cocooned prey.
This is the season when hunger is spun
and abdomens engorge with eggs.
When spiders use their threads
to shelter young, their cycle complete.
An enormity of time
compared to the mayfly's one day,
the baby who's still at birth.

*

The spiders have gone,
the unattached pennants of their webs
floating on wind and their eggs
left in crevices to hatch on their own,
cling to the world with eight legs.
Better to be a moth
and rise above the leveling of earth.
To go from crawling to wings—
a short existence
but one that answers to light.

*

A friend tells me about his daughter
born dead, the umbilical cord
wrapped around her neck
tying her forever to the womb.
He tells me he hears her crying,
sleeps curled into himself
like a fetus waiting for release.
Someone to cup her head, croon

of a mocking bird, a diamond ring
and no matter if the bird can't sing,
the ring doesn't shine.

LOST

I sing around blind curves,
miss my turn and find another world

where dogs have grown tethered to silence.
I begin a new song

they might recognize as the moon
washing light their way

beckoning them to sing along,
the night to beat in three-quarter time.

I step from the car
to waltz among them, kiss each

muzzle as if a prince
might spring from a tangled coat,

reel among the shadows with me,
release his own hushed voice.

Memory of tongues on my cheeks,
shine of eyes as I drive away,

still lost. I uncover birds
that chorus after dark. Roost

within nests of air and praise the stars
undaunted by raptors

as horses doze on their feet.
I climb onto a mare's back,

croon in her ear
of roads leading to wilderness

where horses run free,
never under saddle-weight

or a bit in the mouth.
The mare pricks her ears, whinnies

to the herd surrounded by fences.
At the next fork,

I choose left, greeted by mice
eager to impress,

wooing inaudible to my ear
but enticing to female mice

whose scent inspires such devotion:
chirping and whistling like birds, gibbons,

whales. Off the coast humpbacks
serenading prospective mates, males

taking up the chorus
swelling and ebbing through desire. I sing

around blind curves,
give in to the moon's rise

as fish with silvered scales sound
against the sky, the hum

of a mountain's thrust.
And in the heart of wood,

insects tune their many legs,
psalm like David to his sheep.

A SHORTCUT THROUGH HOLOCAUST

1

Remember carved into the sidewalk:
each camp a figurative arch
a crowd passes under
pausing to read quotes
from survivors, lists of numbers.
A young man hurries on
as if the burden of his backpack
is history enough. He doesn't look
at the quotes, the walls of numbers
but takes the quickest route
through Treblinka, Bergen-Belsen
rather than slow
or choose a different path.

2

I know a woman who walked out
of the Warsaw ghetto,
a girl of six keeping pace with day laborers
leaving for work, yellow stars
pulsing. No one stopped her—
the guards paid to look the other way?
Sometimes mercy rises like light
around a corner: a family friend waiting
to take her in. A man she called uncle,
who raised her Catholic.
Her mother's face melting like hosts,
hands waving her on.
She hid among the lengthening silhouettes
of others, stepped beyond the ghetto gates
and into the world: a slight Polish accent

still tracing her English,
her Christian first name.

3

I follow the young man past milling tourists
to see what awaits: class, work, lover
who makes him forget about time.
But there's just another camp,
more testimonials and numbers.
He weaves his way under arches
and only looks forward,
what's carved in stone
a peripheral distraction, the word *Remember.*

HOW TO TIDY THE WORLD

Sweep all rivers, lakes, seas
under rugs—the brackish in-between.
Let it percolate, salt leaching
through weft and wool. White patches

like the tracings of mollusks
to show where you've been.
Mushrooms beginning to grow
between your toes, ripe as memory.

Polish the sky. Brush away
any clouds, their pale accrual
and dusky lowering. Refuse
to give in to thunder,

which is lightning's voice.
If struck, your blood vessels
may burst in the pattern of fractals.
Branch like trees. Spiral like galaxies.

You are design, endlessly repeating,
and can withstand such bolts
to seize blue. Leaven wind
as if bread. Let its doughy rise enter

through open doors, screen-less windows.
Nothing between you
and what's felt on the face, the tongue—
your eyes tearing, lips chapped.

Strip naked so more of you
can be cleansed. The shadows
beneath breasts, behind knees. Dust
each leaf as it unfurls

into spring's green-gloss. Gather
the hymns of birds and wash them,
song sifting through your fingers
like seed. Brush gravel

to swirl like water's movement
and place boulders as mountains.
Contemplate what you've created
while gleaning night of its stars

and milky footprint
until a purity of darkness remains.
Group constellations on cellar shelves
as if preserves. What can be opened

mid-winter to sweeten the mouth
with light. Clear the gutters
of each season's debris so rain flows
freely. Build an ark where lions lie down

with lambs in a covenant of their own
and you sway with the wild
among you. Wait for the sun's return.
Then rest for a day and begin again.

LETTER SHE WROTE HIM

The singing has started and a hawk kites above fields, intersects sky the way a plane climbs at takeoff then seems to stall—that lull which makes me hold my breath and hope air gives lift. Days lengthen. Trees green bright as flares marking a man overboard: your eyes reflecting water, mine sheltering sun. What I might do with more light while you crave sleep, sail north where night barely grays before dawn and no stars. Stars here, the sky a great camp with its fires lit, and daily the winter wren serenades, body turned to plea. Do you know the origin of mercy? From the Latin *merces—the price paid for something.*

CONFESSION OF A WOMAN TO THE UNLIKELY PRIEST OF WIND

I fear disappearing, mea culpa.
Of turning to dust when touched

as moths do, whose devotion to the moon
is true while I no longer bleed.

Will you bless me? It hurts to kneel
and each night bits of dreams

settle in the corners of my eyes.
What some mistake for sleep

though you know better—
able to lift roofs from houses

and expose the limits of any shelter.
To bead the windows

with a rosary of rain my gaze repeats.
To howl in my stead.

ODE TO BONES

to necks. How they keep each head from lowering
too much but still allow for reverence.
For us to turn toward sound
and what shadows our peripheral vision,
or if stiff, permit only a forward glance
as if warning us not to look back
at the burnt city of our past.
How delicate each vertebrae
on which consciousness rests.
How easily feeling is severed
and we're estranged from our own flesh:
the once familiar house,
door painted red to welcome us in.

*

Ode to spines, thirty-three bones
stacked like a game of Jenga
and collapsing over time so we bend
as if reverting to all fours. We face the ground,
discs bulging white matter
like erupting stars as a sciatic burn radiates
to the toes and nerves jangle like rung bells.
The price for standing erect, learning to speak,
imagining the future.

*

Ode to shoulders, useful for shrugging
in a Gallic manner like the hostess
who can't find our reservation and turns from us
whose names aren't written:
our scapulas rising, chins resting on clavicles
so we resemble neckless souls
hunched in purgatory waiting for release.
When will we be called to break bread,

find our place at the table,
backs straight and blades relaxed?

*

Ode to elbows, seldom attractive,
even on the beautiful, skin wrinkled
and callused from supporting what leans.
And nothing funny about striking them,
an ache like tracing the name on a grave.
A certainty that someday we'll be careless
and injure the pointed parts of us:
unable to nudge ribs and wake those
on either side, direct attention overhead
or thrust our way through a crowd.

*

Ode to wrists that break a fall
and are broken in return.
How even a doorknob can splinter
reaching bones and grips collapse
in a parody of holding on. The numerous hazards:
curbs and escalators, polished floors
slick as black ice. Camouflaged danger
or a moment's inattention
as arms wing to regain balance
and splayed hands take the weight of a body
like a soul its sins.

*

Ode to hips, where we rest our hands
in impatience and other hands rest
to draw us close. Where we widen or narrow
the most. Shelves for groceries and children,
these joints that bruise easily
and distinguish female skeletons from male.
That bear down and hold up.

*

Ode to knees, prone to injury
as if egos reside beneath the patella.
How it's a strain to walk
as bones grind like tectonic plates
and a pressure system lodges in soft tissue
like an approaching storm:
lightning strike of pain,
floodwaters that don't subside.
How we can't change direction, kneel.

*

And ode to ankles negotiating stairs
as we climb and descend, hearts seeking
purchase. As we dream of no harm—
so easy to stumble, so many ways to shatter.

SO MANY DEER

1

Under the apple trees, down on the lawn,
close to the house curled
within their own shadows

as if we're little more than dusk to them
and they're supernatural as the ceramic deer
found in a Mayan king's tomb—

a sculpted figure sitting on its haunches,
front legs raised in supplication
for the spirit to resurrect.

How long have we interceded for the dead?
Looked skyward as if souls burn among the stars,
so numerous, we see by them.

2

Leaves rustle yet no wind.
We hear the deer before we see them,
the sound of hooves placed just so.

We turn to leaf, to branch,
a sanctuary of cedars rising above us,
vaulted sky. The deer leap

like voices onto the lawn,
browse for a time before fading away—
grace never bestowed for long

even when it seeks us
leaving shadows in its place
only the vigilant recognize.

3

A doe and fawn, a road narrowing
between woods. The doe disappears among trees.
The fawn attempts to follow but is lost.

Among your photos, Father, no woods
but many roads where mothers squint
at day's diminishing

and children proffer their hands.
The sun sets on refugees and soldiers.
The sky is a scrim of black and white

though an implication of red—
people prone in dust. I thought
they were sleeping until you told me, no.

A MANNER OF DEVOTION

How we take to the sky in planes
with the promise of wings that won't melt
and to the sea in boats
sealed against water. We trust
that trains will stay on their tracks
and cars remain parallel to each other.
That gravity will tether us to earth
so we don't lose our way
among the silence of space and grow dense
as imploding black holes. That our prayers are heard
before we're brought to our knees.

*

Today, crows alarm as they follow a hawk
to a cedar and position themselves
on either side of it like vigilantes, wary
of the raptor's notion of mercy,
of any creed beyond flight. Earlier this week, a woman
fell like a stunned bird chased into windows.
She collapsed on the street
flailing against exhaust-rimmed snow—
each seizure preceded by light
blinding as an angel's appearance,
each convulsion its own annunciation.
She arched her back and stiffened
as if giving birth. A manner of devotion,
how a man worked a handkerchief
between her teeth like a host,
cushioned her head with his coat
as shepherds knelt in a storefront window.

*

A boy stands at an altar, voice not yet settled
into its pitch. He recites Torah, his sermon
on *Becoming A Man*. But what does that mean?
To broaden with testosterone
and speak in lowered tones?
To shave the chin he hopes isn't weak
and the Adam's apple that can't be swallowed?
To have his measure taken by other men
and beget children whose vulnerability will throb
along his spine, weight nerves
until he can't stand? To be accountable,
chant his portion without hesitation,
only his voice breaking with devotion?

*

Spruce list with moss, daylight deflected
before reaching bark, and drape a trail to the river
that elk seek, split hooves embossed on mud and sand.
Other prints follow, wider than a man's palm.
What pads through forest, nails retracted in patience
as if stalking were prayer, and I recall my shadow
kneeling on pavement, a knife at my throat,
predator's meaty breath. A manner of devotion,
how my assailant knelt too.

*

The ferry churns. City rises on its hills.
We disregard mountains and water, gazes directed

toward phones, disembodied appeals
more comfortable than speech.
Will we revert to hoots and pants,
a language of posturing, the raised fur on our backs
saying it all? Or learn to keen like gulls
while pecking at keyboards?
Even if the ferry founders and we drown,
our devotion reaching into the future—
immortal messages transmitted
as we abandon ship, hearts pulsing like cursors.

*

A crow splays across a pond's frozen surface,
forever fixed as in an Audubon print.
Wind lifts the bird's feathers, grazes its gelled eyes.
Grief clots in furrows like the edges of snow.
A manner of devotion, how Audubon killed his subjects
first then posed them to imitate life,
the crow's beak open mid-caw.
Crows assemble among the cedars and call
and the voice of sorrow is just this—
a crying out with no response
though I repeat your name, gather with others
in dark raiment, sway over an icebound grave.

*

A new season. I dedicate myself to forbearance, to hearing
what Mormon missionaries and Jehovah Witnesses
have to say. My religion not charged with conversion,
a choice between heaven and hell—
my God the Old Testament deity who can turn me to salt
with His white light. As a child, I watched with envy
those who blessed themselves at meals, a devotion
I wanted to borrow, would gladly have eaten fish on Friday—

those pulpy sticks small penance to pay for salvation,
ketchup hemorrhaging on my plate
like the blood of martyrs.

*

Rain in a purging haste beats its tympani
on the roof. Cedars weep, hearts burning
with hoarded light. The wings of birds grow sodden
beyond lift. Have the righteous been warned?
Float with every animal saved
fouling the same watertight space
breathing the same close air, voices silenced
by the untamed among them? In every corner
some creature to be milked, fed, evaded.
Or have lions lain down with lambs
in a devotion of their own?
The sun hides its face like a god.

*

Crows alarm again. Devoted parents,
they have a fledgling to protect
as evangelists shadow my door,
preach of saints and prophesies,
and a sparrow dazed by windows
is placed into a box to recover.
I open it inside rather than test flight outdoors
and the sparrow escapes
to the highest sill, alights eighteen feet up
facing out. Dust floats down, a feather.
The bird beats against glass like bees
trapped in the woodstove, wings laden with soot.
I open windows, doors.
The sparrow huddles on its ledge.
Both of us study the sky.

*

Día de los Muertos, we tend headstones, listen
for phantom voices, leave a rock on each marker
where other rocks rest or lay scattered like stars
where they fell, too numerous to be contained.
We offer food and drink to the dead.
For your family, tamales—
the masa so fine from corn ground by hand
and a fifth of tequila to imbibe
through eternity. For my own, everything kosher—
meat and dairy separate devotions.
We picnic among bones and hope that they rise.
That the buried untangle from mortality's arms
holding them close for minutes or years
and take a seat at the table while we eat—
their spectral hands passing the salt
or cupped around barley soup
as they blow on each mouthful as if making a wish
though what that might be, I never knew.

PAEAN

How I long to see
among dawn flowers,
the face of God.
        ~ Bashō

No burning bush but a flaring
of light that leads to blooms
the color of worship. To recognize
in each leaf my own veining
and in the deer browsing,
the mouthful that sweetens—
my body a purse of blood, flesh
that seeks yield.
How the maples green
despite weeks of freezing rain
and calves lift broad faces
to morning, the fermented grass
of their mothers' milk.
Along the fence, wild roses.

IV.

Instructions
FOR SURVIVING

SQUINTING FITS THE SUN INTO
A CUPPED PALM

and closed eyes conceal what burns.
Yet wind from the south carries a choking haze

so when you say, *let's go north*, I turn
from what smolders and drive on.

No fire where we're headed only rain.
I nod once to acknowledge the prospect

though doubtful any place is free of flame:
our dead already ash and their urns

belted to the backseat like passengers
with bones to break. For 1,200 miles we face forward,

watch for trees to raise the sky with their thrusting,
for water's boundary to draw us toward its edge.

Isn't that what you want, to diffuse memory's char?
Not look over your shoulder and harden to salt?

I WAS A FEARFUL CHILD

The Wizard of Oz with its melting witch terrified me:
its flying monkeys, twister that could leave you
far from home. Dorothy with her little dog,
belief that yellow brick could lead her back.
The hidden wizard and his voice. All those munchkins
with their small bodies pinning me to the ground

like Gulliver among the Lilliputians. Why didn't
my parents understand how real it was to me?
The Snow-White ride at Disneyland
with that witch proffering her poisoned apple.
A waking nightmare, her gnarled hand
reaching out with its wicked gift.
How nowhere was safe because trouble
could strike at any time:

the bogeyman in the closet, monster under the bed,
a bomb as I crouched beneath my school desk.
Few of us remained unscathed,
hearts beating in each other's hands:
the boy who stuttered, face purpling, fists balled;
the girl who didn't speak at all and sucked her thumb

when we made ourselves small avoiding nuclear fallout.
Childhood a looking over the shoulder,
a construct of appeals. If I did my chores
without complaining and kept clean,
no witch would approach me
in the dark with her nightmares,
only the sandman with his bag of dreams.

How I'd descend into reverie's vast bed, pulse
minute as a pinprick of light, large as the slumbering world
and sleep beneath the congealed fire of stars

scattered like the sandman's seed.
My eyelids beating like wings,
I'd kite above any harm though I'm still left breathless

in elevators and marketplaces, on planes and ledges
waiting for metal and stone to give way: list my phobias
as if naming protects against terror. My despair of soaring
only to plunge in a heap broken, the way I fell for you,
not knowing what to call that kind of dread.

IN DREAMS YOU LEAVE ME

and the night grows crowded with men
whose faces I search for some semblance
to yours, some kindness about the mouth.

But the light is dim and these strangers
wear monk-like cowls, close their eyes
in meditation. They turn away

as we circle each other like worlds
existing in parallel but unknown,
the distances too great.

In dreams you return to your first wife—
or some other woman, indifferent to my pleading.
How I beg for your gaze

to recognize me. But you've become impatient
with weeping, roll your eyes,
tsk until your tongue deafens.

I pace hallways empty of any shadow but mine,
study you at breakfast for signs
of that nocturnal persona. Those nights

when your smile becomes a grimace
and you abandon me among men
whose mouths I can't see.

INSTRUCTIONS FOR SURVIVING

Take a feather blue as midnight,
the lunar crescent of its quill,
and decorate a hat with the plume,

use the tip to compose a letter—
its rasping across the page
like the sound of a truth being told.

Remove the spider web
suspended by the door
and swallow any small lives

trapped there, wings beating
against your tongue like words
that should remain unspoken.

Go back to bed and let your pulse slow.
Those who work or attend school
are at their desks

and just a woofing in the distance,
a train. Note the hour.
It always matters when a dog barks

and a train passes with its timetable of faces.
Some person of interest could arrive
at the closest station

and proceed on foot. Few witnesses about
but winter-stripped maples
and they keep their counsel

bared to wind. Listen for glass breaking
as a stranger enters the house and treads lightly
as if approaching a sleeping baby.

Dream the back of a hand grazing your face
is just air, the breath you take in
is your own—each finger about your neck.

THE RODENT INSIDE THE BATHROOM WALL

gnaws at wood or scrabbles to find purchase
and a way back out.
It sounds frantic at times, the wall possessed

and we unnerved as if our bodies have been breached,
flesh shredded to line a nest. You check the roof vents
for penetration

but they're all intact, then discover a hole under the house,
mortar it closed and set traps so the invader,
tempted by peanut butter,

will be snared and no other pests intrude.
Once we found bird seed among summer clothes
stuffed into a guest bedroom dresser.

When we shook out t-shirts
and shorts, seed cascaded onto the floor
as if to take root there,

encourage birds to line the sills
and sing about what lays hidden.
When the cat was alive, we had no such problems.

The smell of her urine discouraged any mouse or rat
from entering. How she kept vigil at windows,
threw herself against glass

if a squirrel or chipmunk came too close,
chattered her teeth, the memory of
incisors crunching through bone.

The rodent inside the bathroom wall
has gone silent, either died within its timber maze
or escaped before its portal was sealed.

When we flush the toilet, it no longer reacts
in a parody of call and response.
Will we smell its desiccated body,

learn to live with the stink of death?
How we're on our own to keep the house intact
from drilling flickers, carpenter ants, termites

that drop from ceiling to bed
as if to pierce the pulpy mass of dreams
and devour our dark centers.

Their appetite invasive as malignant cells
willing to destroy their own vessel,
prove the delusion of any shelter.

SPARROW

Head thrown back, throat opening
to dawn's prelude of light,

song surging in runnels like a tide.
Frost slicks the deck. Last remnants

of snow cling to grass.
The bird won't be dissuaded

from announcing itself.
Always this juggling for territory, a safe nest.

More immigrants approach our borders.
They come in large groups

as if numbers will save them:
cross deserts where ravens follow,

caution the desperate how to circumvent
walls, find a new place to die.

When the sparrow grows still,
and the answering birds,

I suspect a hawk overhead. A shadow
darkening the feeder and driving prey

into windows where there's no escape,
thud of a body against glass.

Quarry stunned or neck broken
as the predator plucks feathers from chests.

Always this division:
those who scan the sky for danger,

those who bring it,
rush of wings like a thrumming of hearts.

CROWS AT THE SUET

Two of them: one watching from the red birdhouse
as the other eats. They caw,
loud as the hard of hearing.

It sounds like an argument about who goes first,
who stands vigil. Always the threat of hawks
overhead and owls as dusk begins to gather.

Every day the crows come as if a mated pair,
eat as if feeding other mouths.
I've grown used to their presence

among the songbirds: black as the memory of night
they carry with them, raucous as a bar fight.
Will others join in? A whole murder of crows

gathered about the suet
like when red wing blackbirds thronged our seed
flashing their bright epaulets and calling

until we took the feeder down, replaced it
with thistle only the beaks of finches could reach.
How good the silence felt. No male black birds

preening their bloody badges like warlords
in countries where food is scarce
and only the strong eat.
No cattail-brown females waiting to feed.

The two crows take turns at the suet
as other birds scatter. They shine in the sun
like wet asphalt, the byways they follow

looking for road kill. A temptation they ignore
for the surety of what we give.
Will they bring us a shiny button in gratitude—

what catches their eye like another sun?
A bit of bone floating in the birdbath.
Unfledged robin from a nest they robbed.

ROOF, GUTTERS, WINDOWS, DECK

No end to what must be maintained.
What grows another layer of moss,

fills with cedar needles, the winging
imprint of birds, fades and splinters.

You treat the deck but leave the ladder work
to those insured against falling.

This is not the time to take risks
when knees and backs have already succumbed

to the weight of years. All those rocks
packed from the beach, even the worm-eaten

that shattered like bone. The wall you built
encircling the apple trees, layers emerging

like a world invoked. How you suffer
from the burden of creation, a sciatic burn

radiating down your leg, its flame licking your spine—
the naked self revealed, so beautiful and terrifying.

*

The men who clean the roof are sure footed
and don't fear falling. They climb ladders

without splintering: know how close to get to the sun
as if buoyed by wings.

Always this division—
those who leave terra firma behind,

those who cling to it. I'd snake, belly to Earth,
rather than risk lift

while you fly in sleep,
kite above each night's little death.

*

The men call to each other
like migrating birds and scrub at metal

as if it were sky made blue again.
Do they dream of flight, of release from gravity's pull?

I dream of tunneling through soil, safe beneath bulwarks
of dirt, my mouth filled with loam.

You take to the heavens, glide on silent wings.
When I hear an owl screech, I burrow deeper,

pull blankets over my head
and wait for my heart to settle.

*

All day the men scrub and polish, sound of their boots
overhead like cedars dropping cones.

Gutters flow freely again. Windows shine.
What birds confuse for light

striking at their reflection, the price paid
for transparency. How perception deceives.

You once dreamed of hurtling through space
in a rocket with convex windows like a fly's eyes

then found yourself wandering
through a museum's narrow halls, your escape

toward infinity thwarted—
past exhibited like artifact behind glass, my face.

*

There's nothing more to be done, everything cleansed
for another year or two

though no telling what will grow inside us.
Time to cull indoors, rid the closets of their detritus.

Those garments long awaiting the embrace of flesh.
Discarded shoes like faithful retainers

preserving the embrace of soles.
Unmatched gloves reaching for hands

and so many coats as if there were doubles of us
to keep warm—even a cape and leather trench

like costumes for roles we once played.
My wedding gown. Your dress blues.

And should you outlive my future gleaning,
I won't relinquish the vacuum or mop

but haunt the house and shadow your every move.
The coolness on your neck, my breath,

the tingling along your jaw, my palms
urging you to lift your head.

For your sorrow would weigh on me like dust
collecting on the dining room table

where you no longer sit
but stand at the counter to eat,

plates heaped in the sink
until I make the faucet drip on the mess.

NIGHTMARE

I choke on my drool, try to slow my pulse
by turning the pillow over to the cool side
taking deep breaths, but fall back to sleep
and into the dream as if never interrupted.
A creature with burnt skin, horns,

forked tail and tongue sits by my side and interviews me
as if for an apprenticeship with evil.
Do you believe in the devil? he asks. In brimstone and fire?
Fear death and any retribution that might follow?
I shake my head no, unable to speak

as he places a clawed hand around my throat
and lightly presses. *No? he repeats*, incredulous
that his existence and his Master's
are negated. How it's possible
to live in the world and not smell its char

even when camouflaged beneath the scent of piety:
candle wax and dust from kneeling.
He relinquishes my throat but sits on my chest
so I feel the density of his body, weight
like a boulder rolled up hill only to tumble down.

An elegant reprimand he wishes he'd thought of
bored with the usual brand of repentance,
the cries of those who'll never see light again.
He imagines punishing with cold not heat. Another ice age
where the sky makes no pretense of sheltering

and there's no longing for eternity or even spring
as colors fade from memory and eyes forget the distinction
between dawn and dusk. Where he'd run blue-nosed

along arctic steppes, seek the imprint of shivering souls:
the loss of paradise nakedness brings.

He decides to be more precise and use a calculus
of transgression to rebuke. Explains to me
how the universe functions mathematically.
Its Golden Mean and Fibonacci sequences
found in the spiral of seeds and galaxies, in the distance

between God's finger and Adam's.
Could he narrow the gap, get there first
and influence behavior?
Cultivate patience like cats and solve problems
while feigning naps, eyes never entirely closed to chance?
I wake again but there's just more night

and the demon waiting as my dream unfolds.
His sulfurous smell fills the room and he smokes
lighting a cigar with his breath, rocks himself
until the bed quakes, chews his nails
until blood banks note diminished supplies.

He's afraid evil is commonplace
and easily surmounted, the good taunting him
with their buoyancy though he appears to those who sleep,
keeps vigil like pets who sense impending death.
He watches for recognition
as heart rates spike before flatlining.

YHWH

G-d's full name too sacred to write
or say aloud, I chant *spoon, fork*
to bring sustenance to my mouth,
intone hands to cup water and repeat Adonai
as a substitute. I watch crows flock
toward their roosts, imagine taking nourishment
from road kill. What leapt too soon or too late—
hind legs still quivering from the effort of flight.
Shadows gather. A dog queries night.
Or is it the stars howling for us
tethered to a darkness only we name?
What sounds like prayer, G-d's abbreviation
etched on wind. What I might taste on wrist and tongue—
learn how to ask for mercy and not slip up.

QUESTION

1

Does memory survive death
as if the great distances between stars,
between one consciousness and another

so we become only thought—
careening points of light
like satellite photos of cities after dark?

Memory still clamoring for attention
like the voices of children. Recollections
kept behind glass

or left to accumulate like old newspapers.
What do we remember best,
smells or faces?

The way eyes fold into themselves,
whiff of furniture polish
overlaid with spent flowers

like churchy confines of an unused parlor
or a bedroom where someone sickened.
Always that odor entering the porch

of your house staying with me
like old skin cells
the nose couldn't shed. A must of cooking

that seeped into fabric
and every room since.
Will it accompany me from life to life

like sourdough starter
while other memories fade
and I'm left to scent my way home?

2

Does memory survive death, the self,
a name? Or is all forgotten but the stink
of a mop left to stiffen and dry?

How smell is the first and last sense
as if we're only a soul
with a nose.

I know nothing of the soul. Whether it enters us
at birth released like lungs into air
and remains with the body

like its shadow or succumbs
when flesh does. How a porch can be
a beginning and an end—

the heady brew of sour cream
and spilled borscht
making me want to die again and again.

WHEN SIZING UP FUTURE LOVERS

Study their hands,
not for any correspondence
between finger length and endowment
but how they'll palm your head
in benediction, cup your face.
Look for a generosity of breadth
and blunt nails that won't raise blood.

Next, turn to their eyes.
Color doesn't matter but whether they remain
heavy lidded with indifference
or shine with self-interest. If so, walk away,
for that will never change
and you'll spend hours searching mirrors
to recover your reflection.

A prospect's mouth also counts,
whether it's open in anticipation
or pursed in judgment, the lips lifted
in a broad or tentative grin. I recommend eager,
yet cautious. A ready smile can be directed at anybody
while an earned one resonates in the stomach
like tolling bells and the thrum of flushed pigeons.

Much is made of chins, for both sexes.
But weak or strong doesn't signify
as much as character. The same goes for height.
A sculpted jaw and tall stature can't always erase
remembered smallness, which may lead to cruelty,
not compassion. Look for relaxed shoulders
and a tenor of mercy in the lower back.

Finally, listen to a lover's voice, their laugh
for instance. Is it uncomplicated as a baby's
or forced? Do you laugh when hearing it,
a release that works unused muscles?
Do you stop and cock your head when they call
your name? Which should sound like bells again,
all of them ringing at once.

RENDITION

with italicized lines
by Pablo Neruda

Railway

I will be waiting for you, as in an empty station
when the trains are parked off somewhere else, asleep.
I'll wear a red blouse bright as a cardinal
in flight and cradle a bouquet of white lilies
like bandages to an open wound. You can't miss me,
the platforms vacant but for a three-legged dog
that sleeps curled around absence and the shifting shadows
of pigeons. What will you bring, a suitcase
filled with books instead of clothes? Something to read
out loud but in translation so nuance is lost?
No matter. We won't have time for subtlety.
Consider my blouse, the lilies and train-less tracks
where I'll linger among pigeons: their eyes
opaque as beads of blood, their need transparent.

Glass

Like a jar you housed infinite tenderness
and the infinite tenderness shattered you like a jar.
I pick through your fractured edges and try not to be cut.
By the mirror, finger bones beckon me
to come closer. In the bathtub, broken ribs reveal your lungs
collapsed beneath the weight of water, your heart
that beats in arrhythmic struggle. And under the faucet
where your spine curls, each vertebrae is bared
like an exoskeleton being shed
and fragments of your skull. Only your jaw remains
hinged: opened wide to express astonishment,

110

its void exposed. But are you really surprised?
The splintering began long ago, the tender crack
in your voice, and long ago you coughed up shards.

Absence

... a house so vast that inside you will pass
through its walls and hang pictures on the air.
You'll call out to hear your own echo,
listen for it down the hall and dream of deserts
like infinite rooms seas once leveled
though water now a mirage as ravens circle
chanting guttural admonitions like prophets.
You'll wake parched and seek my likeness
hung from the sky, drink darkness from my eyes.
There's little else to be done for such thirst
but stir from reveries of loss
and hurl your cup against walls of air.
I'll return balancing a carafe of wine on my head
and throwing handfuls of salt.

Currency

Sometimes a piece of sun burned like a coin
in my hand, like I'd never want for heat and light
and all the shining barter of this world.
You squint at my fist, douse it with water
but still it flares, a dormant star,
blaze seeping through my fingers. A beacon
on days when the sky is lost to cloud

and you wear gloves that resist flame
to cradle my palm: blow on it like a coal
to lift the corners of rooms. Then you suggest
we place the sun's silver among our knives,
unspent. How it gleams like those blades
before they melt and we bury the coin,
buy more knives and sharpen them again.

Aperture

. . . no one saw in my mouth the moon that was bleeding,
no one saw the blood that was rising into the silence.
You take a white shirt and hold it to my lips
to absorb the stain, wring it into dusk
and blot my chin until your shirt becomes a map
of wounded continents. The moon gushes
freely down starched sleeves as I choke
on its red aura while a prediction
of fair weather: an easterly wind
devoid of storm. A sailor's hope lifts
in my chest as night begins to hemorrhage
and I open my mouth and the moon pulses
arterial through shadows
with a radiance that can't be subdued.

ABOUT THE AUTHOR

Sally Albiso earned a BA in Spanish from UCLA and an
MA in English with a creative writing emphasis from
San Diego State University. While at SDSU, she studied
with the poets Glover Davis and Carolyn Forché and
completed a thesis of her own poetry.

After receiving her master's degree, she taught
English composition, creative writing, and English as a
Second Language at Chapman College, San Diego State
University Extension, and Southwestern College.

In 2003, Sally and her husband moved from California to
the North Olympic Peninsula of Washington State, where
she returned to writing poetry.

She has been nominated for two Pushcart Prizes
and received the Jeanne Lohmann Poetry Prize, The
Muriel Craft Bailey Memorial Award, the Robert Frost
Foundation Poetry Award, and the Camber Press
Chapbook Award for her chapbook *Newsworthy*. Two
other chapbooks, *The Notion of Wings* and *The Fire Eater
and the Bearded Lady*, were published by Finishing Line
Press in 2015 and 2016. Her poems have appeared in

Blood Orange Review, Common Ground Review, Crab Creek Review, Floating Bridge Review, Poetica, Pontoon: an anthology of Washington State poets, Rattle, The Comstock Review, and other publications. MoonPath Press published her first full-length collection, *Moonless Grief*, in 2018.

Sally died of pancreatic cancer on October 28th, 2019. Her literary legacy lives on in all her poems and prose, as well as the Sally Albiso Poetry Book Award for Pacific Northwest Poets, endowed by her husband John and sponsored by MoonPath Press.

Made in the USA
Las Vegas, NV
08 July 2023

74385996R00080